Al P..

TRAIN DOGS
The Pack Leader´s Way

Basic Dog Training with Cesar Millan, Karl Lorenz,

B. F. Skinner and Ivan Pavlov

BEGINNER´S WORKBOOK FOR DOG LOVERS

SECOND EDITION
GRAPEVINE BOOKS
2016

ALL RIGHTS RESERVED

TABLE OF CONTENTS

FOREWORD

ABOUT THIS WORKBOOK

"One of my cardinal rules in life is that we must respect animals as the beings they are, rather than as the near-human companions we might wish them to be. To me, having a true bond with an animal means celebrating and honoring its animal nature first, before we start to co-opt it into being our friend, soul mate, or child."

Cesar Millan

AFTER OVER A DECADE OF SUCCESS applying on my own the methods of the Mexican-American dog behaviorist, best-selling author and internationally acclaimed television host Cesar Millan, I decided to prepare this simple BEGINNER´S WORKBOOK FOR DOG LOVERS with the basics of pack leadership and how to effectively apply these when training your dog. This led me to study the main dog-training pioneers and scientific researchers as well as their methods, centering my attention on the pillars dog psychology, positive reward training, classic conditioning and operant conditioning, among other valuable resources widely used by successful trainers.

In sum, *TRAIN DOGS THE PACK LEADER´S WAY* has been especially written to show the beginning student how to become an effective *"pack leader"*, a condition that will certainly help you *"connect"* with your dog and make it easier to train him as well as more effective!

BRIEF STORY OF THESE PAGES

Since 2004 I´ve been a Cesar Millan fan - ever since I saw the premiere of his TV show *"Dog Whisperer"* on the National Geographic Channel that September.

I´d heard that a few years earlier Will Smith and Jada Pinkett, both big dog lovers, had heard of Cesar's special abilities with dogs and asked for his help with some behavior problems they were having with their Rottweilers. Cesar impressed them and the couple started recommending him to their friends. He also Cesar appeared on the Oprah Winfrey Show and eventually got his own show on the National Geographic Channel.

About six months after I saw the premier of "*Dog Whisperer*" I got the chance to attend one of his multimedia live seminars, held at Davisburg, Michigan, which I was visiting on a business trip back in April, 2005.

Like the rest of the participants that attended his seminar that night, I was literally blown away by Cesar´s ability with dogs! He was so much funnier in person than on television and he kept asking us if we understood. No wonder he was considered one of the pet care industry's most recognized and sought-after authority working in the field of dog care and rehabilitation.

During his one-day live seminar, Cesar revealed to us the secrets of happier, healthier relationships between humans and our canine companions in an exciting and entertaining live show. I was inspired by the simplicity of his basic philosophy, which sustains that the secret to happier, healthier relationships between humans and their dogs starts with transforming ourselves. As Cesar explained, for a transformation to take place in a dog, the real transformation quite often needs to take place in us first.

As soon as I got home I tried his training techniques on my Pit Bull Brutus with great results. And since then I have continued studying his methods and have never ceased to apply them. And of course, since then I never miss his TV shows!

A few years passed and I had the chance to see Cesar again when he visited my home state, New York, where he presented a special live event at Rochester's Auditorium Theatre on January 15th, 2012. Once again I witnessed Cesar's extraordinary talent and mastery with dogs.

Today Cesar continues to inspire me as well as countless other dog lovers all over the world. No wonder to this date not only Will Smith and Jada Pinkett, but also Oprah Winfrey, Scarlett Johansson, and Nicolas Cage have all had their dogs trained and balanced by him!

WARNING:

This humble workbook for beginners is not a literal transcription nor a derivative work of the teachings of Cesar Millan, Konrad Lorenz or B. F. Skinner nor does it seek to replace or diminish the sales of their works or to adversely affect their marketability. On the contrary, I highly recommend Lorenz and Skinner's scientific works as well as Cesar's books, TV shows, videos and live seminars for further training!

LESSON 1: BASIC PACK-LEADERSHIP

"The relation of the dog to his master is similar to that of the wolf to the experienced pack-leader which conducts him across unknown territory."

Konrad Lorenz

AS THE MILLENARY IMAGES OF EGYPTIAN DOGS show, back in ancient times trained dogs and canine trainers were common in the land of the pyramids. In fact, representations of working dogs can not only be found the imagery of ancient Egypt but also of Mesopotamia, Greece, Persia, and Rome, where trained dogs were commonly used as hunting, guard, police and war dogs, as well as household pets.

The oldest written reference of dog training dates back to the year 127 BC, when the octogenarian Roman farmer and author Marcus Terentius Varro wrote in Latin his *"Three Books son Farming"* (*"Rerum Rusticarum Libri Tres"*). Apart from other matters, he included advice on raising and training puppies for herding livestock, not only recognizing the value of early training but also describing specific methods for specific tasks.

It is said that Varro wrote many books, but most were destroyed by the Romans when he was forcefully exiled as an old man. Only his trilogy on farming, due to its undisputed popularity, managed to survive in complete form. Curiously, he started to write these books in his *"eightieth year"*, after his wife, Fundania, repeatedly told him he was no *"spring chicken"* and that he should *"summarize his knowledge of agriculture."*

Throughout the centuries that followed, countless dog-training methods have been used, grouped worldwide. However, they can be reduced to two different mainstreams: those based on rewards (recommended) and those based on punishment (not recommended). Unfortunately, for thousands of years and until recent decades, most animal trainers based their methods on harsh punishment.

Pack leadership, among other methods, is based on positive reward training, owing its original roots to the studies of the Austrian zoologist Konrad Lorenz and the 1800s pioneers of positive reward training. Today, after being perfected by Cesar Millan, pack leadership constitutes one of the world's most popular and reliable training methods …and the movement still grows!

PACK LEADERSHIP AND DOG PSYCHOLOGY

The fundamental basis of successful pack leadership is a clear understanding of dog psychology and how it operates.

According to Cesar Millan, dog psychology stresses the importance of understanding our dogs *"from a dog′s point of view"*. According to him, most people make the mistake of treating dogs like humans, forgetting that no matter what you think or believe your dog is just that: A dog!

As he explains:

"The more you learn about dog psychology, the better you will be able to connect with your canine companion."

But, what is dog psychology?

And how does it work?

Cesar defines dog psychology as:

"The science of understanding dogs from a canine perspective rather than from a human perspective."

Dog psychology is based on the knowledge that dogs (as well horses and elephants among other pack mammals) live in small groups and follow their natural group leaders. Its study includes two differentiated main branches:

**Psychological studies of dogs in their natural packs*

**Psychological studies of dogs living with humans*

The following sums up some of the main findings regarding these two branches:

PSYCHOLOGY OF DOGS IN THEIR PACKS:

*Most wolves and wild dogs live in natural groups or packs (although not all wolves live in groups and some do not live in groups all year round).

*Wolf packs and wild dog packs are led by one or more dominant leaders followed by a group of submissive individuals.

*In the case of wolf and wild dog packs, the pack leaders control the other members of the pack and set the rules.

*Pack leaders don't project anxiety, tension nor fear. They calmly and assertively project security to the pack.

*Dogs are instinctive. They basically need to eat, a place to sleep and a pack to keep safe.

*There can only be so many pack leaders in a pack, so most dogs are submissive by nature, creating harmonious social balance.

PSYCHOLOGY OF DOGS LIVING WITH HUMANS:

*When you adopt a dog and bring it home, you and your family become part of his family group or symbolical "*pack*".

*Giving him love alone unbalances your dog´s behavior. Dogs also need a leader they can trust and follow!

*Dogs need discipline, so be sure to train your dog to obey the rules, boundaries and limitations you impose.

*Dogs also need exercise, so make sure your dog gets all the exercise he needs or at least take him out and walk him every morning for at least 45 minutes.

*Your dog always picks up your feelings of fear, anxiety, rage, confusion, pain or worry. So remember to keep it cool and at ease whenever you re with your dog. Be the pack leader!

*To minimize your dog's anxiety, only reward him when he is in a calm state. Let him earn his reward! Once he is calm, you can reward him and give him all your love.

*Your dog looks like a dog, walks like a dog and thinks like a dog. It's not human! So don't expect from him more than he can give!

*The more you learn about dog psychology, the better you will be able to connect with your canine companion!

CESAR'S FULFILMENT FORMULA

Dogs are mammals that respond to calm-assertive leadership, not to intellectual reasoning nor emotional arguments or negotiations. So, if you have a dog, keep in mind Cesar's fulfillment formula:

> *"Dogs have found themselves in an odd*
> *predicament by living with humans. In the*
> *wild, dogs don't need humans to achieve*

balance. They have a pack leader, work for food, and travel with the pack. But when we bring them into our world, we need to help them achieve balance by fulfilling their needs as nature intended them to be.

"How does this work? Through my fulfillment formula: exercise, then discipline, and finally, affection. As the human pack leader, you must set rules, boundaries, and limitations and always project a calm-assertive energy. When you fulfill your dog on a primal level as nature intended, you will feel in tune with your dog and connect with your dog in a deeper way. Put your dog's needs first, and take responsibility for our dog's state of mind. Only then will you experience all the love your dog has to give!"

IMPORTANCE OF CONDITIONING

Since ancient times dog training has depended on the correct application of the principles of what are presently known as *"classic conditioning"* and *"operant conditioning"*.

Used for thousands of years, the correct application of these principles can allow you to improve your dog's behavior according to your personal needs or desires, as shown in the following pages …so read on!

LESSON 2: CLASSIC CONDITIONING

IVAN PAVLOV (1849-1936)

"The nervous system is the most complex and delicate instrument on our planet, by means of which relations, connections are established between the numerous parts of the organism, as well as between the organism, as a highly complex system, and the innumerable, external influences."

Ivan Pavlov

THE KEY NATURAL LEARNING PROCESS that allowed the rise of dog training in ancient times was first described by the Russian physician and researcher Ivan Pavlov, Nobel Prize winner in 1904. Known for his systematic study of the basic laws of the *"learning process of dogs"*, he was the first to vital define the role of what he called *"conditioning"* or *"conditioned training"*.

Applied since ancient times by animal trainers, *"conditioning"* is defined as *"the act or process of training a person or animal to do something or to behave in a certain way in a particular situation"* *(Merriam-Webster)*.

A dog is said to be conditioned when he learns to respond automatically to a new *"stimulus"* by adopting the same *"acquired behavior"*.

Determined to solve the profound mystery behind the dog´s *"basic non-conscious instinctual type of learning"*, Pavlov set up a series of revolutionary experiments with canines in his St. Petersburg laboratory. And he claimed success!

The following are the basics of the process of *"classic conditioning"* as Pavlov first described around a century ago and some examples of how you can effectively apply his findings when training your dog:

PAVLOV'S CLASSIC EXPERIMENT

Pavlov's *"classic"* scientific experiment with dogs took place in Russia's Imperial Institute of Experimental Medicine and went as follows:

The first part of the experiment involved a four basic steps repeated several times a day, for a few days:

1: A dog was hooked to a mechanism that measured the amount of saliva he produced.

2: A bell rang just before the dog was fed.

3: The amount of saliva produced increased with the sight of the food.

4: The dog ate freely and without interruption.

The same process was repeated each time the dog ate, two or three times a day. After several days of repetition and reinforcement, the *"conditioning"* took place.

The second and final part of Pavlov's experiment served to evidence that the "conditioning" had indeed taken place.

The same dog was hooked to the same mechanism to measure the amount of saliva he produced and then a bell rang.

But this time no food was brought and the dog was not fed!

However, the dog salivated instinctively to the sound of the bell alone as if their food had actually been served!

Following the process of "*conditioning*", Pavlov concluded, the dog had actually "*learned*" by repetitive "*training*" to salivate to the sound of the bell alone, just like our mouths water at the site, smell, or even the mention of our favorite food.

BASIC COMPONENTS OF CONDITIONING

After analyzing the results of his historic experiment, Pavlov identified the four basic components of conditioning, which serve as basis of his classic behavioral model:

*The unconditioned stimulus is the stimulus that naturally and instinctively triggers the response, in this case food.

*The unconditioned response is the natural reaction to the unconditioned stimulus or food, that is, salivation.

*The conditioned stimulus is the new stimulus artificially introduced to trigger the response, in this case the bell Pavlov used in his experiment.

*The conditioned response is the natural reaction to the new conditioned stimulus. In his experiment, Pavlov found no reaction in the beginning but in the end the dogs produced salivation in response to the sound of the bell.

And thus, Pavlov's simple experiment with dogs served to describe the basics of an automatic and nonconscious learning process that affects the behavior of both animals and humans.

APPLYING CLASSIC CONDITIONING

Dog trainers can benefit in many ways from applying principles of classic or Pavlovian conditioning. For example, when teaching your dog how to interpret hand and voice signals in his basic training:

Voice signals

Just like the bell in Pavlov´s experiment, single-word voice signals or commands can be used to trigger specific responses in your dog. Try to always use one-word commands and always pronounce the voice signal with the same tone and inflection after gaining your dog's attention by saying his name. The most common are "sit", "come", "stay", and "lie down", among others, later described"

When you start out training your dog, teach him one command at a time. Practice it many times and once he learns it, teach him another one and then practice the two and so on. Don't get carried away with the number of commands you teach him. Take it easy!

Hand signals

You can also use conditioning to teach your dog to obey different hand signals. In this case, instead of Pavlov′s bell a specific position of the hand will trigger a desired response.

Among the most common hand signals is placing your flat hand over and in front of your dog′s head while saying "sit" before pulling it up into a loose fist. Another common practice is placing your left hand above your dog's head, palm toward the floor, and then lowering your hand towards the floor while saying "down".

In any case, using a specific hand motion can be an effective way of training a dog to respond to different stimuli.

When training your dog, start out by using voice and hand signal commands and eventually you can wean your dog off the vocal command so that he responds to the hand signal alone. This is most useful for giving long-distance orders Cesar recommends giving hand signals in front of and above the dog's head for that is where his best field of vision is.

TAKING CONDITIONING A STEP FURTHER

Although Pavlov's theory was promptly accepted by scientists worldwide, some particular researchers found it was too simplistic and did not serve to explain more complex animal and human behaviors.

Pavlov's attempt to force behavior into the simple stimulus-response formula simply didn´t seem to work in large scale.

This led to further scientific research and animal experimentation, finally leading the way to the development of what came to be known as *"operant conditioning"*.

This new and improved behavioral model now described, step by step, the process followed when reinforcing a specific behavior or diminishing it and also outlined the specific steps you need to take to modify your dog's behavior, as revealed in our next lesson!

LESSON 3: OPERANT CONDITIONING

B. F. SKINNER (1904-1990)

"The kind of behavior that is correlated with specific eliciting stimuli may be called respondent behavior and a given correlation a respondent. The term is intended to carry the sense of a relation to a prior event. Such behavior as is not under this kind of control I shall call operant and any specific example an operant. The term refers to a posterior event..."

B. F. Skinner

CONSIDERED THE BASIS OF ANIMAL TRAINING, the process of "*operant conditioning*" was first outlined by the Pennsylvanian psychologist and behaviorist Burrhus F. Skinner, (1904–1990), who considered Ivan Pavlov′s classical conditioning too simplistic to explain complex behaviors,.

In his revealing 1938 study of animal and human conduct, "*The behavior of organisms*", Skinner criticized the simplicity of Pavlov's classic model before setting the formal basis of "*operant conditioning*":

> "*With the discovery of the stimulus and the collection of a large number of specific relationships of stimulus and response, it came to be assumed by many writers that all behavior would be accounted for in this way as soon as the appropriate stimuli could be identified.*

> "*Many elaborate attempts have been made to establish the plausibility of this assumption, but they have not, I believe, proved convincing...*

> "*I do not believe that the stimulus' leading to the elaborate responses of singing a song or of painting a picture can be regarded as the mere substitute for a*

stimulus or a group of stimuli which originally elicited these responses or their component parts...

"The attempt to force behavior into the simple stimulus-response formula has delayed the adequate treatment of that large part of behavior which cannot be shown to be under the control of eliciting stimuli. It will be highly important to recognize the existence of this separate field in the present work.

"Differences between the two kinds of behavior will accumulate throughout the book, and I shall not argue the distinction here at any length.

"The kind of behavior that is correlated with specific eliciting stimuli may be called respondent behavior and a given correlation a respondent. The term is intended to carry the sense of a relation to a prior event. Such behavior as is not under this kind of control I shall call operant and any specific example an

operant. The term refers to a posterior event, to be noted shortly..."

Taking Pavlov's theory a step further, Skinner based his research on discovering the basic principles of the conditioning that regulates animal and human conducts and determine how specific behaviors can be increased or decreased.

Also known as the father of *"operant conditioning"*, Skinner explained what is considered the basis of animal training since ancient times, something you as your dog's trainer and leader should definitely be familiar with!

Skinner based his model on two basic modifiers of human and animal conduct.

*Reinforcers

*Punishments.

Although Skinner was openly against the use of harsh punishment, his model includes what he called *"positive"* and *"negative"* punishments. Presently most dog trainers are against the use of physical violence and never recommend it. Fortunately, this detestable practice has lost strength in recent decades, a gradual process that curiously began in the late 1800s, many years before Skinner and Pavlov, when the world's first dog-training books were published by the pioneers of *Positive Reward Training*, as the following chapter details.

POSITIVE AND NEGATIVE REINFORCERS

According to Skinner, there are two types of reinforcers: positive and negative, as explained below.

POSITIVE REINFORCERS:

Positive reinforcers modify your dog's behavior by offering him a *"favorable reward or outcome"* each time he behaves properly. In order to be effective, however, the reward must be given immediately after the desired behavior. For example, by praising and rewarding your dog each time he obeys a new command, he will be more likely to repeat the same behavior in the near future.

The most common rewards for dog are praise, food, petting and hugging, among others. Regarding the use of food when rewarding your dog, Skinner pointed out in *"The behavior of organisms"*:

> *"A conditioned alimentary reflex is easily established in a hungry dog but slowly or not at all in one recently fed."*

NEGATIVE REINFORCERS:

Negative reinforcers does not involve punishment. They consist in the removal of an unfavorable or unpleasant outcome if your dog behaves properly. For example, a dog that obeys commands to avoid being punished. Sometimes, however, negative reinforcers backfire. Suppose your dog wants out, for example, and he starts barking loudly near the front door, like always. If you give in and open the door for him (like he wants), of course your dog will stop barking and leave! But by doing this, you will actually be reinforcing his loud barking and excited behavior each time he wants out!

In sum, when used properly, positive and negative reinforcers can both increase the likelihood that a specific behavior will later be repeated by your dog!

POSITIVE AND NEGATIVE PUNISHMENTS

Positive and negative punishments are used to make a dog less likely to repeat an unwanted behavior. They are just the opposite of positive and negative reinforcers, for they weaken or eliminate a specific behavior instead of strengthening it. Correction

POSITIVE PUNISHMENT:

Though I don't recommend the use of physical violence nor hurting animals in any possible way, it consists in giving your dog a disciplinary punishment, for example a spanking to weaken his undesired behavior. In certain cases you can use mild non-violent punishments to discipline your dog, as later described.

NEGATIVE PUNISHMENT:

Negative punishment, on the other hand, consists in removing a favorable reward to weaken your dog's undesired behavior. For example, taking away your dog's favorite toy following an undesired behavior will surely help decrease that behavior.

VOLUNTARY AND INVOLUNTARY CONDITIONING

As Cesar Millan recommends, be always alert when you're with your dog because whether you realize it or not, you are always conditioning his behavior. Truth is, your dog is always paying attention to your verbal and non-verbal language, even if you are not!

For example, if you walk your dog and always get nervous when walking by big dogs, you will in fact train him to also be nervous. And if you get excited and run to the door every time the bell rings, you are actually training your dog to also get excited and run or jump around each time he hears that bell ring!

No matter what you do, even unknowingly, your dog will always pick it up! So keep in mind Skinner's basic principles and be aware of the effects of voluntary and involuntary conditioning for, as we shall see in the following pages, you can always use these to your best convenience when training your dog! So read on!

LESSON 4: POSITIVE REWARD TRAINING

"Common sense shows that you ought not to correct your dog for disobedience, unless you are certain that he knows his fault."

W. N. Hutchinson

STARTING IN THE MID-1800s, a group of experienced British and American dog trainers published the world's firs dog training books, describing the olden methods used at the time including those based on positive rewards, which publicly rejecting the use of harsh physical punishment, thus setting the basis of what came to be known as the "*Positive Reward Training*" movement, still alive today.

Among its most respected pioneers, the following canine trainers stood out:

W. N. HUTCHINSON

In 1848 the British Army officer and Governor of Bermuda Lieut-Gen W. N. Hutchinson (1803-1895) published one of the world's first dog-training books under a most extensive title: "*Dog Breaking: The Most Expeditious, Certain and Easy Method, Whether Great Excellence or Only Mediocrity Be Required, With Odds and Ends for Those Who Love the Dog and the Gun.*"

Primarily concerned with training hunting dogs such as pointers and setters, Hutchinson favors a form of reward-based training, dedicated to men who have "*a strong arm and a hard heart to punish, but no temper and no head to instruct*".

Hutchinson is considered the precursor of Positive Reward Training, which minimizes the use of punishment as Hutchinson suggested:

"Be to his virtues ever kind. Be to his faults a little blind."

In his celebrated book, for example, Hutchinson gives out the following advice to help you correct your dog for disobedience:

"Common sense shows that you ought not to correct your dog for disobedience, unless you are certain that he knows his fault. Now you will see that the initiatory lessons I recommended must give him that knowledge, for they explain to him the meaning of almost all the signs and words of command you will have to employ when shooting.

"That knowledge, too, is imparted by a system of rewards, not punishments. Your object is not to break his spirit, but his self-will. With his obedience you gain his affection.

"The greatest hardship admissible, in this early stage of his education, is a strong jerk of the check-cord (leash), and a sound rating, given, when necessary, in the loudest tone and sternest manner ; and it is singular how soon he will discriminate

31

between the reproving term 'bad' (to which he will sensitively attach a feeling of shame), and the encouraging word 'good,' expressions that will hereafter have a powerful influence over him, especially if he be of a gentle, timid disposition.

"In educating such a dog, and there are many of the kind, likely to turn out well, if they are judiciously managed, often possessing noses so exquisite (perhaps I ought to say cautious), as nearly to make up for their general want of constitution and powers of endurance: it is satisfactory to think that all these lessons can be inculcated without in the slightest degree depressing his spirit.

"On the contrary, increasing observation and intelligence will gradually banish his shyness and distrust of his own powers; for he will be sensible that he is becoming more and more capable of comprehending your wishes, and therefore less likely to err and be punished."

STEPHEN HAMMOND

In 1882, the American dog trainer and author Stephen Hammond, editor of Forest and Stream magazine, published his book "*Practical Dog Training*", recommending that dogs should always be praised and rewarded with meat when they perform the correct behavior.

Regarding this reward method, Hammond recommended the following in the pages of "*Practical Dog Training*":

> "*We think it a very good plan to always have in our pocket something good for him to eat, and when he minds this long note and comes in quickly, we reward him with a bit of something substantial as well as with fine words.*

> "*This system of rewards must not be carried too far nor practiced too often, but used occasionally when he performs his duties in a satisfactory manner; especially when he comes in at the sound of the whistle quickly and cheerfully, a little piece of meat will at least have no tendency to slacken his speed when next he hears this signal.*

"This instantaneous, almost electric obedience and cheerful alacrity is most pleasing to witness, especially when hunting in company with others whose dogs may not be quite up to the standard in this respect. Therefore no pains should be spared to so perfect our pupil in this, so that when we come to practical work in the field his actions shall cause us no disquiet nor reflect discredit upon our skill as his teacher.

COLONEL KONRAD MOST

In spite of the efforts of those who favored positive reinforcement methods, many renowned 20th Century dog trainers recommended the use of unnecessary compulsive practices as the spiked collar, forced compliance and the switch. Among these stands out the German police officer and dog trainer, Colonel Conrad Most, principal of the *"State Breeding and Training Establishment"* for police dogs in Berlin, who in 1910 published his *"Training Dogs: A Manual"*, which wasn't translated into English until the year of his death, 1954.

Other than his system of punishment, despised by contemporary dog trainers, Col. Most is recognized for having introduced new behavioral training principles that were considered *"revolutionary"* at the time, many of which are still applied by military and police dog trainers worldwide.

By the time his manual reached America, Col. Most's book was already an European best-seller. During the Second World War he had headed the Nazi *"Experimental Institute for Armed Forces' Dogs"* and, after the war, presided the *"German Dog Farm"*, a training center for working dogs, including help for the blind. He also stood among the founders of the *"German Canine Research Society"* and the *"Society for Animal Psychology."*

PACK LEADER REWARDING

The use of food rewards (especially meat and dog biscuits) is one of the oldest known techniques in dog training, widely used since ancient times.

This effective technique is based on simple conditioning and is highly effective, but only if you apply it immediately after your dog adopts a desired conduct to correctly condition his behavior.

When dog treats are used properly, they can become a powerful tool for motivating your dog during training and accelerating the desired results. For example, if you reward your dog with a treat every time he does something specific right, you will be reinforcing that specific behavior for the future. And that's precisely how many dogs are successfully trained.

Although Cesar's techniques include the use of treats as positive reinforcements, they don't always mean treats your dog can eat. Petting on the head or back and praising, for example, can also be used as operational rewards as well as giving him his back his favorite toy.

In any case, the use of proper rewards in dog training have proven to be effective for counter-conditioning methods, that is, for re-teaching your dog certain behaviors.

For example, if you dog doesn't like his crate you can leave its door open and place some food treats inside. Do this several times until your dog associates the crate with dog treats and he will stop disliking it.

According to Cesar, *"giving your dog treats is more than an expression of love for our dog; it can be a critical component in dog training and rewarding good dog behavior. Always use treats to reinforce a calm, submissive state and never to reward excited, over-stimulated states of mind."*

CESAR'S TREAT GIVING TECHNIQUE

Cesar recommends the following technique for giving treats:

FIRST:

Hold the treat in your hand between the first two fingers and the thumb. Let your dog sniff so that she knows it is there, and remember my rule: nose first, then eyes, then ears! When you engage your dog's nose, you are appealing to the most important part of her brain.

SECOND

Next, as she is sniffing and getting interested, slowly lift the treat above nose height and move it gradually over her head and slightly back towards her shoulders. The aim is for your dog to lift her head up, move her shoulders back, and naturally have her butt lower to the floor.

THIRD:

Lift the treat slowly and easily so that your dog's nose follows it in your hand. If she jumps at your hand, take it away. Next time, have the treat hand closer to her head. The moment she begins to follow the treat with her nose and eyes and her butt beings to move to the floor, say, "sit," calmly and easily, and give her the treat. Use a natural voice as you don't want to startle or distract her.

Keep in mind what Cesar says:

> *"One of my cardinal rules for training is*
> *don't overexcite your dog so that she loses*
> *the lesson in all the commotion."*

LESSON 5: THE FATHER OF PACK LEADERSHIP

KONRAD LORENZ (1903-1989)

"The dependence of a dog on his master has two quite distinct origins; it is largely due to a lifelong maintenance of those ties which bind the young wild dog to its mother, but which in the domestic dog remain part of a lifelong preservation of youthful characters. The other root of fidelity arises from the pack loyalty which binds the wild dog to the pack-leader or, respectively from the affection which the individual members of the pack feel for each other."

Konrad Lorenz

WHAT IS PRESENTLY KNOWN AS "PACK LEADERSHIP" originally derived from the writings of the Austrian zoologist, animal behaviorist and founder of ethological research Konrad Lorenz, author of *"King Solomon's Ring"* (1949) and *"Man Meets Dog"* (1950).

Pack leadership was more recently developed by contemporary researchers and dog trainers, including Cesar Millan, who perfected it, giving it its present form.

The original version of pack leadership was based on Lorenz's view of the role of natural leaders in wolf packs, as he described in *"Man Meets Dog"*:

> *"In order to obtain enough nourishment for its large requirements, the wolf pack is obliged to cover great distances, when the members must support each other staunchly in their attacks on big game. An exacting social organization, true loyalty to the pack-leader and the absolute mutual support of all its members are the conditions for success in the hard struggle for existence of this species.*
>
> *"These properties of the wolf explain without any doubt the very noticeable difference in disposition between jackal*

and Lupus dogs, while is quite apparent to people with a real understanding of dogs. While the former treat their masters as parent animals, the latter see them more in the light of pack-leaders and their behavior towards them is correspondingly different."

Regarding what he called *"the dependence of a dog on his master"*, Lorenz stated in his book:

"The dependence of a dog on his master has two quite distinct origins; it is largely due to a lifelong maintenance of those ties which bind the young wild dog to its mother, but which in the domestic dog remain part of a lifelong preservation of youthful characters. The other root of fidelity arises from the pack loyalty which binds the wild dog to the pack-leader or, respectively from the affection which the individual members of the pack feel for each other."

Lorenz recommended using positive rewards and avoiding the use of violent physical punishment, favoring other ways of reprimanding dogs, as described in *"Man Meets Dog"*:

"To begin with, the question of reward and punishment; it is a fundamental error to consider the latter more efficacious than the former. Many branches of canine education particularly 'house-training' are much better instilled without the aid of punishment.

The best way to 'house-train' a newly acquired young dog of about three months is to watch him constantly during his first few hours in your house and to interrupt him the moment he seems likely to deposit a corpus delicti of either liquid or solid consistency.

"Carry him as quickly as possible outside and set him down, always in the same place. When he has done what is required of him praise and caress him as though he had performed a positive act of heroism. A puppy treated like this very soon learns what is meant, and if he is taken out regularly, there will soon be nothing more to clean up.

"The most important thing is that punishment should follow an offence as quickly as possible. There is no sense in beating a dog even a few minutes after he has done something wrong, since he cannot understand the connection.

"Only in the case of habitual offenders which are quite conscious of their misdoings is delayed punishment likely to be of any use. There are, of course, exceptions to this rule: on the occasions when a dog of mine has killed a new animal of my collection simply out of ignorance, I have been able to impress upon him the enormity of his conduct by hitting him later with the corpse.

"This was not so much calculated to imbue the dog with the wrongness of a certain deed as to fill him with revulsion for a certain object. As I shall describe later I have resorted in certain cases to 'prophylactic punishment' in order to inculcate in the dogs a feeling for the sanctity of new house-mates.

THE "PACK-LEADER" CONTROVERSY

When Lorenz introduced the original *"pack-leader"* theory he believed that wolf and dog packs were rigid, military-like societies. But scientific research long proved that this is not so.

Among other mistakes found in Lorenz's original theory, a 2010 research by the University of Parma and the Rome Veterinary Hospital evidenced that dog packs don't necessarily have a single leader, that different dogs can occasionally hold the role of pack-leader and that, in most cases, the pack-leaders are not necessarily the most aggressive nor dominant members, but its oldest.

In any case, the true essence of Lorenz's theory remained untouched.

It presently constitutes the basis of what is considered one of the most world's most popular dog training methods.

Its opponents claim that the term *"pack-leader"* cannot refer to a human. But I personally believe that when used in dog training it is strictly a *"metaphoric"* or *"symbolic"* term that should not be understood literally.

Of course humans cannot be TRUE pack leaders because they are not dogs! And of course they cannot ACTUALLY be part of canine packs! That's obvious! But I don't believe this means we should definitely drop the term *"pack leader"*, as one of its harshest critics Victoria Stilwell recommends in her book, *"Train Your Dog Positively"*:

> *"... It is time, therefore, to finally retire the term pack leader – especially when it refers to humans interacting with dogs. Domestic dogs don't live in true packs, and even if they did, we, as a different species, wouldn't be a part of them."*

However, the polemic continues. In spite the fact that many dog trainers and researchers are openly in favor of pack-leader training, unfortunately there are many who are openly against it.

BASIC PRINCIPLES OF PACK LEADERSHIP

When Cesar Millan perfected the theoretical basis of pack leadership, he included the following ten basic principles, among others:

*Since dogs are pack animals; your dog will either lead or follow.

*Dogs follow calm and assertive energy, not excited energy.

*Love alone cannot not balance your dog's life. You need to be a pack leader!

*More than love and affection, your dog needs exercise, direction, and clear leadership.

*Always practice your leadership. The energy you internally project is the message your pet will receive.

*Always walk your dog in the morning and let him know you lead.

*Your dog need discipline, so don't forget to give him rules, boundaries, and limitations as well as love.

*Dogs seek their pack leader for stability and accept the pack leader's role with natural submission.

*Dogs are not humans; humanizing your dog is your biggest mistake.

*It takes dogs a few seconds to know your role: leader or follower.

LESSON 6: CLAIMING LEADERSHIP

"The walk establishes you as your dog's pack leader and is instrumental to your dog's state of mind. While on the walk, the dog walks calmly at your side (almost like a heel position or slightly behind) and never in front."

Cesar Millan

TO BEGIN TO ESTABLISH YOURSELF as your dog's pack leader keep in mind the following recommendations:

1: ACT LIKE A LEADER: Adopt a leading role at all times. Make your dog know that you are his leader and, as such, are always in charge and in control.

2: CONTROL YOUR VOICE: Always use a clear, strong voice when commanding your dog. Avoid shouting.

3: SET CLEAR RULES: Set rules, boundaries, and limitations. Dogs need to follow rules to keep calm, not excited nor dominant.

4: KEEP A CALM, ASSERTIVE ENERGY: Dogs follow calm, assertive leaders, as Cesar stresses, leaders capable of building strong and balanced relationships with their pet.

5: REFUSE TO BE DOMINATED: You know your dog dominates you when he jumps on you, barks at you or gets you to do what he wants even if you don't want to! You can also tell if he dominates you by seeing if he always pulls your leash when you walk him and likes to walk in front. Refuse to be dominated! Be a pack leader!

6: LEARN TO GIVE AFFECTION: Cesar points out that people tend to give affection at wrong times, when their dogs are afraid, excited or angry. For example, if we get home and our dog jumps around with excitement and hug or caress him while saying nice things we are actually reinforcing this behavior and get him more excited. Instead we need to teach our dog that we will give him affection only once he calms down and adopts a submissive state, that is, only once he earns it!

CLAIMING THE LEADING ROLE

To symbolically claim and take over the role of your dog´s pack leader you basically have to clearly establish that you´re the boss.

Cesar Millan is able to do this within minutes of meeting a dog and without using physical force, as seen on his celebrated TV shows.

But how does he actually do this?

There are many "ways" to claim the pack leader role. Here are five he often uses that have also worked for me and my dog:

1: CLAIM HIS FAVORITE SPOT

Only pack leaders are able to successfully claim a territory and keep it. So one way of taking over the pack leader role is to let your dog know that you are in control of your home´s physical space. All of it!

The fastest way to let the dog know that you´re the leader is to claim his favorite spots.

It doesn't matter if it's the front porch, the living room sofa, or a kitchen corner. Look for a favorite spot and follow these instructions:

1: Wait until your dog goes to a favorite spot.

2: Walk up to him, and gently move him away and take over the spot. Simply sit there or stand next to it.

3: The dog will naturally try to return to his spot, even if you are there too. Block him with your legs or hands and keep him away, no need to say a word. Just push him away, don't let him get near. And don't use physical force.

As a pack leader you have the right to claim your territory and control all the space within your own home. If not, then your dog will always be in control of your house/space.

Body blocks prevent your dog from moving in certain direction or from stepping into a particular space. Extending your leg or arm in front of the dog to prevent him from moving forward will do.

You can accompany this with the "tsch" sound and finger poking, if needed. You need to let your dog know it's not "his" place any more.

4: After a while, the dog will calm down and understand that you, his master and his pack leader, are superior than him and in control. Then he will "surrender" to you submissively by either lying down or sitting nearby in a calm way, waiting for you to decide what's next.

5: Once he does this, it is always good to praise him and reward him with a doggie treat or by giving him a favorite toy. Of course, part of the reward is also giving him back his space.

6: Do this several times a day for several days.

II: CLAIM HIS FAVORITE FOOD

1: Place your dog's food plate in front of you. Preferably with a favorite food.

2: As soon as your dog walks to the plate, stop him from getting near it only by using your legs (body blocking). Let him know you are in control and that the food plate is yours, not his. But don't say anything or use hand signals. Simply, each time your dog tries to get near his food plate correct him by body blocking him and making him to move back. To do this extend one leg forward and place it in front of the dog to stop him and then the other if he moves sideways and insists.

3: Stay near the plate at all times, blocking your dog every time your dog wants to get near his plate until he surrenders. He will finally accept your superiority as pack leader and will surrender and relax, waiting for your next step. Most probably, your dog will sit or lie nearby without even trying to get near you or his plate unless you let him.

4: Once he "surrenders", it is always good to praise him and reward him with a doggie treat or by giving him a favorite toy. Of course, part of the reward is also giving him back his space.

5: Do this several times a day for several days.

III: CLAIM HIS FAVORITE TOY

1: Wait till your dog plays with his favorite toy or one of his favorites.

2: Walk up to him, and gently take the toy away from him and stay there, showing it to him.

3: The dog will naturally try to reach for the toy but don't let him. Raise it high in the air, where he can see it but can't reach it. You can accompany this with the "tsch" sound. You need to let your dog know it's not "his" toy any more. It's yours!

4: After a while, the dog will calm down and understand that you are his pack leader and therefore in control. Then he will "surrender" to you submissively by either lying down or sitting nearby in a calm way, waiting for you to decide what's next.

5: Once he does this, it is always good to praise him and reward him with a doggie treat. Of course, part of the reward is also giving him back his toy.

6: Do this several times a day for several days.

IV: CLAIM THE FRONT DOOR

You should always be the first one out the front door and the first one in –no exceptions. Only pack leaders are able to freely enter or leave your house. Your dog will need to learn that he simply can't run out of the house each time you open the door. And the fastest way to do this is by following these steps:

1: Stand with your dog in front of or near the front door (it also works for the back door and any door).

2: Walk up to the door or stretch your arm, and gently open the door wide.

3: As soon as he sees the open door, your dog will naturally take a run for it and head to the door. If he doesn't then in his case there's no need for this exercise.

4: Don't say a word. When he approaches the door, block him with your legs and stop him from reaching it and place yourself in front of the door, claiming it. The dog will probably insist and maybe try to run between your legs or through one side. Continue blocking him with your legs in complete silence, preventing him from reaching the door. Try to push him away, don't let him get near. But don't use physical force.

5: After a few minutes, the dog will calm down. He will accept that you are superior and in control. And then he will "surrender" to you by either sitting or standing in front of the door where you are standing.

5: Once your dog relaxes, it is always good to praise him and reward him with a doggie treat or by giving him a favorite toy. Of course, part of the reward is also letting him out freely through the door.

6: Do this several times a day for several days.

V: LEAD HIS WALKS

Cesar recommends dedicating at least 45 minutes to your dog's walk each morning. According to him, leash walking is a great way to let your dog know that you are in charge and establish yourself as his pack leader because it gives you the chance to lead him.

Your dog needs to know that walking is not really up to him, it's up to you. In other words, you bring your dog to the situation; your dog doesn't bring you.

To successfully do this, keep in mind the following steps:

1: Assume the role of a real canine pack leader and keep quiet. You do not need to speak to your dog as you walk.

2: Try to always walk in front of or beside your dog. This will allow you to be seen as the pack leader. But if your dog takes the lead, then it will mean to him that he is controlling you on the walk, and that he's the pack leader instead of you. This is also why you should always be the first one out the front door and the first one in. Your dog should be beside or behind you during the walk.

3: Instead of giving your dog verbal commands, command him through the leash and through your body language. For example: If your dog moves ahead of you and pulls on the leash, you need to immediately do a light leash jerk to make him stop, that is, you need to pull up on the leash. That´s why Cesar recommends using short leashes.

4: It has to be a quick jerk or a snap (not a tug). Its force should always be to the side, rather than directly back. And then the leash should be loose again. Cesar normally uses leash jerks when walking a dog with a leash. Especially when the dog tries to walk in front of him or pulls on his leash. Also when the pet needs to concentrate in walking and not in his surroundings or in other dogs. According to Cesar, these jerks helps to "center" the dog´s attention and get it "back in place".

5: Cesar´s advice is to always correct, and then relax. Once you've given the correction with the leash, your dog should be able to do what he's supposed to do with no need of verbal or hand commands. And by doing this you will establish yourself as the pack leader, the one in command. Therefore, the walk will not only work him out physically but also balance and relax him psychologically.

According to the American dog trainer and Cesar Millan fan, Judy Huston:

> *"The walk establishes you as your dog's pack leader and is instrumental to your dog's state of mind. While on the walk, the dog walks calmly at your side (almost like a heel position or slightly behind) and never in front.*

> *"During this walk, there is no need to even talk to your dog. They get into the zone of walking and enjoying the process very quickly. This step is critical to the entire process."*

LESSON 7: MARKS AND NO-MARKS

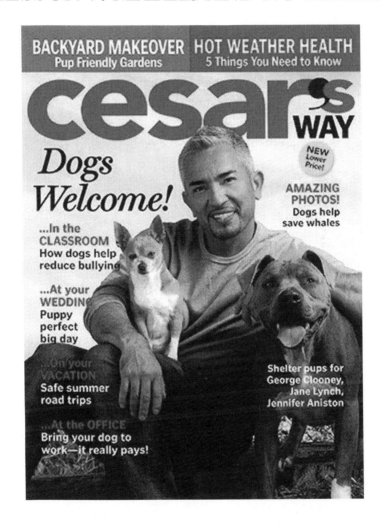

"*Many dogs grow up without rules or boundaries. They need exercise, discipline and affection in that order.*

Cesar Millan

IN HIS TV SHOWS WE HAVE SEEN Cesar Millan *"punishing dogs"* without really hurting them. And this is something his opponents have always criticized.

But as Cesar explains, those are simple *"no-marks"* he is trying to establish and his training or rehabilitating methods have never included hitting or really hurting the dog. In fact, he never even raises his voice to the dogs! And, truth is, he really doesn't need to.

THE USE OF MARKS AND NO-MARKS

Cesar recommends applying the principles of *"operant conditioning"* to modify your dog's behavior positively with the use of what is known as *"marks"* and *"no marks"*.

A **mark** should be used when your dog does something right.

A **no-mark** should be used when your dog does something wrong.

Characteristics of marks and no-marks

The following are the main characteristics of marks and no-marks used by dog trainers all over the world, including Cesar Millan:

*A mark doesn't need to be verbal.

Mo-marks" are not intended to really hurt the dog.

You can use different marks and no-marks to indicate different degrees of rightness and wrongness.

Each dog trainer can develop and use his or her own marks and no-marks.

You can use artificial devices, such as bells, whistles or keys to generate a "unique sound" to mark or no-mark dog behaviors.

Let's say, for example, that Cesar is dealing with a dog who is always on the sofa and never lets anyone else sit on the sofa. Evidently, the dog is assuming the role of the pack leader because his owners aren't.

Cesar would take the dog off the sofa or have one of the family members do it, and then he would "claim" or take possession of the sofa by not letting the dog anywhere near. He would probably sit on the sofa, and each time the dog came near him, he would poke him with his finger and say the word tsch. Or he would block the dog with his legs and even use his foot to gently tap or slap the flank of the dog.

CESAR'S BASIC MARKS AND NO-MARKS

If you've seen Cesar's shows, you'll probably know that he never really hits or hurts the dogs when punishing them. Instead, he uses the "no-marks" described in the following pages, which you should always use whenever your dog does something wrong.

The tsch sound

If you're familiar with his shows, then you've probably heard his "tsch sound", a consistent verbal no-mark he uses when a dog is misbehaving.

By conditioning, you can teach your dog to associate the tsch sound with punishment. For example, if you use the tsch sound when he misbehaves and nevertheless your dog continues misbehaving, you can follow-up the no-mark with some negative action like finger poking or time-out, among other light punishments described in these pages.

By doing this your dog will understand that if a no-mark is ignored there will be unwanted consequences. These consequences, however, don't always need to be physical. Instead, it is more effective to take away one of your dogs most valued resources, like his freedom. For example, if he is misbehaving with a guest, then take away his access to the guest until he calms down and behaves.

In any case, due to the increasing number of Cesar Millan fans, the "tsch" sound is becoming a universal language that everyone does and understands.

It is most effective when used jointly with finger poking.

Finger poking

Finger poking is a simple method of correction consisting of a light but firm poke in your dog's neck or chest area (rib cage) using two fingers and simulating the poking of a fellow canine.

Finger poking can be used for correction or simply to "snap your dog out of something".

Remember: Finger poking doesn't have to be hard enough to hurt the dog.

As Cesar explains, this is simply what other dogs do when a dog is acting inappropriately: they poke him with their noses!

Finger poking is most effective when used jointly with the "tsch" sound. Eventually, however, just the "tsch" sound is all you will need to stop a dog behavior you don't like.

Also, apart from finger poking, Cesar sometimes uses his foot to gently tap the flank of the dog for correction.

Body blocks.

As we saw before, this technique is used to limit your dog's space and freedom.

Never forget that as a pack leader you have the right to claim your territory and control all the space within your own home. If not, then your dog will always be in control of your house/space.

Body blocks prevent your dog from moving in certain direction or from stepping into a particular space. Extending your leg in front of the dog to prevent him from moving forward will do.

Cesar recommends body blocks for claiming the role of pack leader, as well as for keeping your dog from rushing out of your house without permission, stepping into a specific space within the house (could be your bed or the sofa) and when you don't want your dog crowding you, among other cases.

No contact rule

When meeting a new dog, Cesar always recommends the no talk, no touch, no eye contact rule, also known as the no-contact rule. You can also use it when your dog is overly excited or overly seeking for attention until he calms down. This is how it goes:

You pay no attention to the dog until he is in a calm, submissive state. Only then you can pet him and praise him as a reward for being in a calm, submissive state.

The no contact rule works well, but can be hard to follow.

Some people can't avoid giving a dog eye contact, especially if the dog is so excited and happy to see them. But you must do it in order to let him know that you are in control and that he needs to calm down.

The no contact rule is most useful when contacting a hyperactive dog. Simply ignore his behavior. Dogs want your attention. By paying attention to them you're reinforcing their behavior. By ignoring them till they calm down, you reinforce their calmness. See the difference?

So the next time your dog is jumping around like crazy or nipping at you overexcitedly, use the no contact rule and see what happens. Remember: no touch, no talk, and no eye contact. You'll be surprised with how quickly your dog settles down!

Time out

The time out technique is a lite punishment that consists in removing your dog from where he presently is and taking him to an "extremely low stimulus area" and leaving him there until he calms down.

For example, you can take him to your basement, back yard or laundry room, as long as it is an "extremely low stimulus area", taking away his freedom and his external stimuli until he calms down.

A firm command to sit or lie down when you leave him there can also help your dog relieve some of his tension and cool off.

Light leash jerks

Cesar normally uses light leash jerks when walking a dog with a leash. Especially when the dog needs to concentrate in walking and not in his surroundings or in other dogs.

According to him, these jerks helps to get the dog′s attention "back in place".

It has to be a quick jerk or a snap (not a tug). Its force should always be to the side, rather than directly back. And then the leash should be loose again.

CESAR′S NO-MARKS IN ACTION

For those of you who haven′t seen Cesar′s TV shows, I must explain that he widely uses all the no-marks just described in this lesson.

Those who have seen his shows know that Cesar constantly uses the "tsch" sound and finger poking to control dogs and modify their behavior. In fact, he uses the "tsch" sound and finger poking in one of the "Ghost Whisperer" episodes described by the English-Canadian journalist and bestselling author Malcolm Gladwell in his May 22, 2006 article for *The New Yorker*:

IT TAKES TIME & PRACTICE

According to the American dog trainer and author Sylvia Cochran, *"it takes time and effort to see real improvement in your dog's behavior; don't let your frustrations distract you from your goal to properly and successfully train your pet"*.

Cochran recommends following Cesar's advice and starting out by setting boundaries in your home. For example, if your dog does not respect your private space work on this issue when training. Or if your dog's barking annoys you, work on this instead:

> *"You must have unwavering mental strength and confidence to gain the trust and respect of your dog during training sessions. Your dog can sense if you are uncertain or fear it, so you must control situations by maintaining the role of an authoritative pack leader.*

> *"It takes a household to properly train a dog. You, your partner and all household members need to be on the same page when it comes to acceptable and unacceptable behavior. While there only is one pack leader, the other family members still are*

dominant to the dog, and they must treat their relationship with it as such.

"It never is too early or too late to start working with a dog. Whether your canine companion is a puppy or a more mature dog, commit to start today and achieve with your dog what Millan refers to as balance between people and dogs."

LESSON 8: BASIC DOG COMMANDS

"To the accompanying order of 'Lie down' or other appropriate words which the trainer has decided to use; a certain amount of force may be necessary the first time the order is given. Some dogs understand the command earlier, others later, and still others stand stiff as a wooden horse and only begin to grasp the situation when first their hind-legs and then their fore-legs are bent under them by force."

Konrad Lorenz

NOW THAT YOU HAVE LEARNED the basic methods of the pack leader's way, you're ready to teach your dog some basic commands.

PLANNING YOUR TRAINING SESSION

These are some basic recommendations when training your dog and teaching him new commands:

*Keep your training sessions short. You can start out with sessions from five to fifteen minutes maximum.

*Make sure your dog pays attention to you before starting the session. If he does, reward him with food treats as well as praising and petting.

*Speak always with firm voice, never with fear, anger nor over-excitedly.

*Always end your sessions with a reward.

*If possible, train from puppyhood. Puppies are more responsive to new commands and will learn quicker. However, despite the fact that older dogs may require more time and patience, consistent reward training will also do the job.

*Be always firm and secure, displaying your leadership.

*Feel free to use Cesar′s "marks" and "no marks" and remember: A **mark** should be used when your dog does something right. A **no-mark** should be used when your dog does something wrong. The recommended marks are doggie treats, praising and petting. And the recommended no-marks are the tsch sound, finger poking, body blocks, the no contact rule and time out.

DON′T OVERLOAD YOUR DOG

It′s best to take it easy and don′t overload the dog. According to the professional dog trainer and animal welfare writer Sally Gutteridge, inexperienced dog trainers can often place unmanageable demands on a dog:

"In professional and properly educated dog training, situations care is taken to keep the dog happy and the training undemanding. By asking too much of any dog, the trainer knows that he will simply over faze it.

"A good and effective dog trainer will know the dog's personal limits. The excellent trainer will teach a dog something in careful stages keeping canine confidence high and setting the dog up for success throughout.

"Dogs that are offered a reward which makes them happy, whether in the form of food or a toy are motivated to learn. It has been proven repeatedly that dogs learn the best when they have prior knowledge of a desired reward."

As a preview of the second book of this series, *DOG TRICKS THE PACK LEADER'S WAY*, in which I expand on this matter, here are some of the most common dog commands your pet should know:

THE BASIC COMMANDS

There are many reasons for pet owners to want a calm, obedient and faithful dog. For one thing, obedient and trained dogs are happier dogs, less likely to get into tussles with people or with other dogs. Another reason is that many human communities require that the dogs living in their neighborhoods be well trained.

This is especially true for many breeds thought to have aggression and behavior problems, such as Rottweilers or Pit Bulls, like my own dog Brutus. Of course, basic training will also make your dog a much better companion -especially in households where there are young children.

Many studies have also shown that proper dog training makes a big impact when it comes to cutting down behavior problems. When considering training your own dog, or having someone else help you train it, there are certain basic commands that must be mastered in order for a dog to be considered truly trained.

The basic obedience commands that every dog must know are:

*Come

*Sit

*Stay

*Heel

*No

*Down

*Off

*Stop

*Stop & Sit

These commands form the basis of basic obedience training, and it is vital that you and your dog master these commands.

These are the fundamentals. And it will be impossible to move onto more complicated commands, or to correct behavior problems without first mastering the basic commands.

THE COME COMMAND

IT IS IMPORTANT that all dogs learn to go to their owners upon command. Therefore the first training command you need to teach your dog is the come command.

As we shall see, teaching your dog this basic command is essential for him to learn and it can be used for various different reasons. For example, if you take your dog for a walk and you let him off the leash, then you can expect him to come back to you, instead of running around the park with you chasing after him shouting "Get back here!" or "Come back, Fido!"

That would be just downright embarrassing!

Especially because to teach your dog how to come at will only requires basic conditioning techniques and some repetition. But it's really quite simple, as we shall now see.

Basic steps to follow

The simplest way of conditioning your dog to obey the "Come" command requires you to take the following steps:

*Get a toy in one hand and a treat in the other.

*Simply walk by your dog or walk away from him-

*Then hold out the toy and excitingly say the command "Come!"

*When your dog comes to you, give him a treat.

*Do this several times a day and always use the same command for come.

*In two or three days he will have learned to obey your command.

Remember: This is a great way to teach him, but don't forget to have lots of long breaks so he doesn't get bored and stop enjoying it... and don't forget giving him treats!

Things to consider during this training

Coming when called is a vital skill that every dog must learn, both for its own safety and that of those around it.

A disobedient dog that refuses to come when called could easily be hit by a car, get into a fight with another dog, or suffer a variety of other bad experiences. A well trained dog that comes when called can safely be taken out to play in the local park, at the beach, on the hiking trail, or anywhere else the owner and dog may wish to go.

Basic training to come when called is relatively easy and straightforward, and involves providing praise, treats and other perks when the dog does as his owner wants.

After these basic come when called training exercises are mastered, there are a number of fun exercises that can be introduced to challenge the dog and pique its interest.

One thing to avoid is following the "Come" command with unpleasant, hurtful or menacing activities.

Calling your dog, and then immediately giving him a bath, clipping his nails, taking him to the vet, etc. will quickly teach the dog that coming to the owner has negative consequences.

It is best to ask the dog to come and then reward him, pet him, play with him, feed him, walk him or engage in other fun activities.

If you do need to take your dog to the vet, bathe him, etc. be sure to allow some time to pass so the dog does not associate the "Come" command with the bad experience. It is also important to remember that dogs are constantly learning, whether a formal training session is in process or not.

Your dog is always learning something from you, whether good or bad. It is therefore important to make every interaction with your dog a positive one.

When teaching the dog to come on command, it is vital that the dog be consistently rewarded every single time he does as the owner wants.

A reward can be as simple as a pat on the head, a "good boy" or a scratch behind the ears. Of course, treat based rewards are appreciated as well, and many dogs are highly food motivated and respond quickly to this type of training. The key is to be consistent. The dog should get some kind of reward, whether it is praise, a toy, or a treat, every time he appears at the owner's side when called.

Refusing to come when called

Many dog owners fail to recognize the importance of having a dog that comes when called until there is a problem, such as the collar or leash breaking, or the dog tearing free to chase a person or another animal.

These situations can be dangerous for the dog, the owner and other members of the community. In areas where there is a lot of vehicular traffic, the situation could even prove fatal to the dog.

Unfortunately, many well-meaning owners sabotage this important part of their dog's training by allowing it to run off leash and unattended. Whether the dog is allowed to run in the park, on the beach, or just play with other dogs, this teaches the dog that there are many fun things that do not involve its owner. In fact, from the dog's perspective at least, these fun times are often ruined by the appearance of the owner.

Look at things from the dog's perspective for a moment.

You —the dog— is having a ton of fun running on the beach with all your doggy friends, and suddenly here comes this human to take you away from the fun. When you see the dog's point of view it is easy to see how the appearance of the owner and the leash can be seen as a negative. This negative perception causes many dogs to delay this outcome by refusing to come when they are called.

From the dog's point of view, this makes perfect sense, since every minute of delay means another minute of romping on the beach or in the park. In other words, the dog has learned that the most rewarding thing to do is to ignore the calls of its owner.

While this may seem like a good idea to the dog, it is definitely not a good thing from the owner's perspective.

For dogs who have not yet learned this type of avoidance behavior, it is best to prevent it from happening by supervising the dog at play, and making the time you spend with your dog as much, or more, fun, as the time it spends alone or with other dogs. For dogs that have already learned the value of ignoring their owner, some retraining is definitely in order. It is vital that every dog respond to the "Come" command, for the safety of both humans and dogs alike.

THE SIT COMMAND

The sit command is a vital link in the chain of dog training.

Teaching a dog to sit on command, using voice commands alone, will form the groundwork of much future training, so it is important for the dog to master this vital skill.

Getting your dog to sit is a bit harder than getting him to come. But not that much. Again, it only requires basic dog conditioning and repetition. Once you have mastered the "Come" command, follow these steps to teach your dog to sit:

*Call your dog to you using the come command.

*Place your hand on the end of his back (lower back) and say the command "SIT".

*Gently push down on his backside until he sits.

*Give him a doggie treat and a lot of praise. If you want him to sit longer just delay giving him the treat and the praise, get him to sit but take your time bending down to him and feeding him his tidbit.

THE STAY COMMAND

Like the sit command, the stay command is a vital building block to other, more advanced training. For instance, the stay command is vital to teaching the dog to come when called, which is in turn vital to leash work.

The stay command can be made into an extension of the sit command.

*Have your dog sit, and while he is sitting, slowly back away.

*If the dog begins to follow you, as he probably will it first, come back to the dog and ask him to sit again.

*Repeat the process until you can reach the end of the leash without your dog getting up from a sitting position.

*After the dog is reliably staying where you indicate, you can try dropping the leash and backing further away.

*It will probably take the dog some time to reliably stay where he is put without becoming distracted.

THE NO COMMAND

The word "No" is an important one for your dog to learn, and one you may be using a lot as training begins.

It is important that the dog learn to respond to a sharp "No" promptly and obediently.

To train your dog to obey this command, you can use the different "no-mark" techniques recommended by Cesar, including the "tsch" sound, hand poking, and body blocking, among others.

THE HEEL COMMAND

One of the most basic commands of all is the "Heel" command.

Teaching a dog to heel is one of the first steps in teaching the dog to walk properly on the leash. The proper place for the dog to walk is at your side, neither lagging behind nor straining to get ahead.

*If your dog begins to forge ahead on the lead, gently tug on the leash. This will cause the training collar to tighten and give the dog a gentle reminder to fall back into line.

*If you dog begins to lag behind, gently urge him forward. A lure or toy is a good tool for the dog that constantly lags behind.

*Once the dog is consistently walking at your side, try to change your pace and encouraging the dog to match his pace with yours.

*It should always be the dog who adjusts his pace to you; you should never adjust your pace to meet the needs of the dog.

THE OFF COMMAND

The "*Off*" command is just as vital to as the other commands, as it forms the basis for later training, especially when training the dog not to chase people, cars, bikes, cats, etc.

For instance, when training a dog to remain still when a bicycle goes by, the owner would stand with the dog calmly on the leash.

If the dog begins to strain against the leash, the owner sharply issues an "Off" command accompanied by a tug of the leash.

Eventually the dog will learn to respond to the voice command alone.

THE BASKET COMMAND

The father of pack leadership Konrad Lorenz describes what he called the basket command as follows in his book *"Man Meets Dog"*:

> *"One may easily find the dog in the way and want to get rid of him for a time. The command 'Go away' is one that even the cleverest dog cannot understand, since 'away' is an abstract which he is quite unable to apprehend; one must tell him in a more concrete way whither one wishes him to go.*

"The basket need not be a real one, but only means a fixed place to which the dog is made to retire on order, and which he must not leave without being told. It is best to choose some corner for which the dog has already shown a preference and to which he will always go willingly.

"Children and dogs can make themselves very unpopular by disturbing the conversation of adult people and a dog that has learned to leave people alone will certainly earn general approval."

APPENDIX: CESAR'S EARLY YEARS

William Morris Endeavor (WMA)

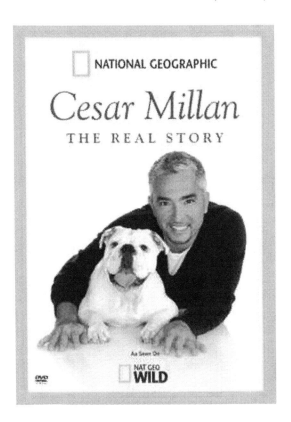

MILLAN WAS BORN IN RURAL CULIACAN, MEXICO,
and grew up in a small house with no amenities. He spent much of
his early childhood on his grandfather's farm in nearby Ixpalino,
where he observed the behavior of the farm's many dogs.

When he was a teenager, his family purchased their first TV. He
preferred the classic "Lassie" and "The Adventures of Rin Tin

Tin" series and, inspired by them, decided that he would move to California and become the world's best dog trainer.

In December of 1990, at the age of 21, Millan, who spoke no English, crossed the border and began living in San Diego. He lived on the streets for a month until he got a job grooming dogs, soon gaining a reputation for his easy way with even the most difficult dogs. With a few dollars in his pocket, he moved north to Los Angeles and took a job washing cars.

During this time, Millan was surprised by how troubled so many of the dogs he encountered seemed to be. He began thinking that he should redirect his dream to becoming a *rehabilitator* rather than trainer of dogs.

With the money he saved from washing cars, he started a freelance dog rehabilitation service, primarily offering his expertise with extreme cases. He was quickly recommended around town and his client list expanded rapidly. In 1994, he came to the attention of Will Smith and Jada Pinkett Smith who likewise referred him to other celebrities.

That same year, Millan married his wife Ilusion who inspired him to upgrade his business and reach further into the community. Together they opened the Dog Psychology Center, a two-acre facility in South Los Angeles, expressly to rehabilitate troubled, aggressive, and condemned dogs. He usually keeps a pack of thirty to forty "unadoptable" and abandoned dogs at the center.

CESAR'S TV DEBUT

In 2002, Millan was profiled in the *Los Angeles Times*. Los Angeles-based production company partners Jim Milio, Melissa Jo Peltier, and Mark Hufnail of MPH Entertainment, with their colleagues at Emery/Sumner Productions, called upon Millan with the idea of creating a TV series with him, with no commitment from any network.

MPH, a multi-award winning production company that discovered and executive produced the hit film *My Big Fat Greek Wedding*, next developed and filmed a 'pilot' show entitled "Dog Whisperer with Cesar Millan," and sold it to the National Geographic Channel, where it became the cable network's top rated series its first season.

In April of 2005, Millan, his wife Ilusion, and MPH Entertainment teamed up to create Cesar Millan, Inc. (CMI). It is the umbrella organization that develops, creates, and manages all of the enterprises associated with Millan, including television shows, books, DVD releases, CDs, seminars, and branded products.

Millan has a partnership for the design, creation, and sales of his own proprietary line of dog products with PETCO since July 2008. These include organic dog food, olfactory toys, natural treats, leashes, ergonomic collars, and specially designed, breed-specific beds, among other items.

A POP CULTURE ICON

Today, Millan has become a pop culture icon, inspiring flattering parodies on "South Park" and "Saturday Night Live;" references on popular shows including "Jeopardy!" and "Two and a Half Men," appearances on "Oprah," "Tonight Show with Jay Leno," "Martha Stewart," "Carson Daly," "Today Show," "The View," "Nightline," "World News Tonight," "The Morning Show with Mike and Juliet," and "Live with Regis and Kelly;" as well as cameo roles on the hit series "Ghost Whisperer" and "Bones."

Millan has worked with many celebrity clients including: Charlize Theron, Scarlett Johansson, Oprah Winfrey, Nicolas Cage, Michael Eisner, Scott Rudin, S.I. Newhouse, Ridley Scott, Rebecca Romijn, Michael Bay, Hillary and Haylie Duff, Denise Richards, and Vin Diesel. He has been recognized with numerous awards throughout his career.

In 2005, the National Humane Society Genesis Award Committee presented him with a Special Commendation for his work in rehabilitating animals; in 2006 and 2007 *Dog Whisperer with Cesar Millan*" was nominated for an Emmy for Outstanding Reality Program.

ALL RIGHTS RESERVED

GRAPEVINE BOOKS

Made in the USA
Middletown, DE
28 December 2017